Who Is
David Beckham?

by Ellen Labrecque

illustrated by John Hinderliter

Penguin Workshop

For Ethan and Brady Cosgrove—EL

To Niko, a Plum boy who loves to
be on the soccer field—JH

PENGUIN WORKSHOP
An Imprint of Penguin Random House LLC, New York

Text copyright © 2020 by Ellen Labrecque. Illustrations copyright © 2020 by Penguin Random House LLC. All rights reserved. Published by Penguin Workshop, an imprint of Penguin Random House LLC, New York. PENGUIN and PENGUIN WORKSHOP are trademarks of Penguin Books Ltd. WHO HQ & Design is a registered trademark of Penguin Random House LLC. Printed in the USA.

Visit us online at www.penguinrandomhouse.com.

Library of Congress Control Number: 2019054585

ISBN 9780399544040 (paperback)   10 9 8 7 6 5 4
ISBN 9780399544064 (library binding)   10 9 8 7 6 5 4 3 2 1

Contents

Who Is David Beckham?

Five-year-old David Beckham was as excited as if it were Christmas morning! It was September 6, 1980, and his dad, Ted, was taking him to watch his first professional soccer game. They were going to see Manchester United—one of the most popular sports teams in the world. United was playing Tottenham Hotspur. The two were teams in the English Premier League—the top professional soccer league in England. David and his dad drove to Tottenham's stadium, about twenty-five minutes from their home in Chingford. David wore his favorite red United jersey. When they entered the giant stadium, David gripped his dad's hand tightly. They were both so excited for the game, they had arrived very early. They were two of the first fans there.

Their seats were high above the field, far from the action, but David didn't care. He loved every minute of the game. He loved the loud cheering of the fans, and the way the soccer ball moved quickly from player to player. The game ended in a 0–0 tie. David didn't get to see any goals, but he had the time of his young life.

"I'd never seen him more thrilled," Ted said about his son. "To see his face light up had been worth the price of the tickets alone."

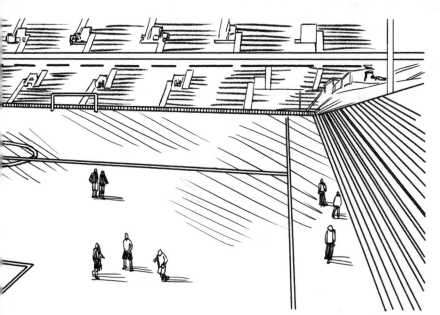

As they left the game, Ted carried his son down the steep stadium stairs. David turned to his father and said, "Dad, one day I am going to play for Manchester United." Ted laughed and responded, "I'll come and watch you."

When David said this, his dad didn't really believe him. After all, only the very best players play professional soccer—and only the best of the best play for Manchester United. But David meant it. And from that day on, he worked as hard as he could to make it happen. Growing up, he spent almost every hour he could practicing soccer. Every day, every year, he got better and better.

David Beckham became one of the best and most famous soccer players ever. He played eleven seasons for Manchester United, four

seasons for Real Madrid in Spain, six seasons for the Los Angeles Galaxy in California, and one season for Paris Saint-Germain in France. He also played for fourteen years on England's national team.

David became a multimillionaire, married a pop star, and became famous for his cool clothes, good looks, and hip hairstyles. But before *any* of these things happened, David was just a little kid who held his dad's hand during the matches. He loved soccer more than anything else in the world.

CHAPTER 1
Born to Play Soccer

David Robert Joseph Beckham was born on May 2, 1975, in northeast London, England. His mother, Sandra Georgina, was a hairdresser, and his father, David Edward Alan Beckham—known as "Ted"—installed new kitchens. David was a middle child. He had an older sister named Lynne Georgina.

Shortly after David was born, his family moved to Chingford, a suburb ten miles from London.

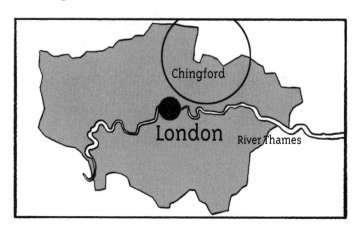

Chingford had plenty of grassy parks and open space for kids to play sports, especially soccer.

Soccer is called *football* in most parts of the world, including England. English people are especially obsessed with soccer. They love to play it, watch it, and talk about it any chance they get. David's father, and soon David, loved soccer, too.

When David learned to walk, his father brought him to a local park almost daily for a "kickabout," or to kick the soccer ball around. Ted also bought his son a soccer uniform and a new ball for Christmas every year. As David got older, Ted taught his son all the skills he needed to play the game.

"We would work on passing, crossing, and shooting, for hours and hours," David said.

David was a small boy, but he was a natural athlete. He was way better at soccer than any other child his age, so he played against older kids instead. Sometimes David even practiced with a local team on which his dad played.

The World Loves Soccer!

Soccer is the world's most popular sport. There are more than 265 million people around the world who play the game and 3.5 billion people who call themselves soccer or football fans. The sport was first played in England, and a match was first

described in a book written in 1174. English explorers spread the sport to other parts of the world.

Perhaps one of the reasons soccer is so popular is because it is inexpensive to play: All you need is a ball and some goal markers to kick the ball through.

The men on the team were three times as tall, three times as heavy, and three times as old as David. When the bigger guys knocked him down, David's dad told him, "Get up and get on with it."

By the time he was seven, David had a baby sister named Joanne Louise. His days were filled with soccer. If he wasn't playing in the park or practicing with his dad's team, he was playing on his own teams. His bedroom walls were covered with posters of famous soccer stars, especially players on Manchester United, his favorite team.

"All I ever wanted to do was kick a football about," David has said. "It didn't enter my head to do anything else."

David was shy and quiet, but he had a warm and easy smile. He wasn't a great student. He spent a lot of time in the classroom daydreaming of one day being a professional player. The one class David did well in was art. He was excellent at drawing. Most of his sketches were cartoons of soccer players and games.

David also enjoyed getting dressed up in his good clothes—not something you'd expect from such an athletic boy. But as young as seven, David had an interest in the latest styles and in men's fashion. "He loved looking smart and all his clothes had to match," David's dad remembered about his son. "If you suggested he put *blue* trousers with a *red* shirt, he would go mad."

David's parents saw an advertisement that read "Wanted: Football Stars of the Future" in the local newspaper. A man was starting an under-eight youth travel soccer team and was looking for players. David, who already played on his school team, jumped at a chance to be part of another squad. Forty-three kids showed up to the tryouts, and only eighteen made the team.

Ridgeway Rovers, 1985

David was one of them. The team, called the Ridgeway Rovers, practiced almost every day and traveled as far away as Germany and Holland to play in youth tournaments. This might have been too much soccer for some of the players, but not for David. He loved every minute of it. And he quickly became the star of the team.

"Even at age eight he could hit the ball from every corner of the pitch," said David's Rovers coach. "He could strike the ball like a rocket—from any distance. He was a slight boy and I feared he wasn't going to be strong enough—but his skills won through."

David played on the Rovers for six years. His dad even became one of the assistant coaches. The coaches ran the Rovers like a professional team.

The boys all had to wear sweaters and ties when they traveled to away games. When they played, their cleats had to be completely clean before the start of every match.

Most of the boys didn't like getting dressed up, but David did.

"Right from the start, we tried to make it as professional a setup as possible," explained David's dad, "and I'm sure that paid off. It certainly did for David. It showed him how important it was to be properly prepared."

When David played, his dad was tough on him. If he thought his son played a bad game, he told him so.

Sometimes David cried when his dad told him he played like "rubbish." But Ted also told his son exactly what he had done wrong. This way, David could fix his mistakes the next game. David understood his dad just wanted him to get better. Later David would even say to his father, "Dad, you were right, you know."

Then Ted and David would sit down to watch something on the telly—usually another soccer game.

US vs. UK English

People in the United Kingdom (UK) speak English, just as people in the United States (US) do. But they sometimes use different words (and, of course, a British accent!).

United Kingdom	United States
Biscuit	Cookie
Chips	French fries
Football	Soccer
Gobsmacked	Totally surprised
Holiday	Vacation
Jumper	Sweater
Lad	Boy
Mum	Mom
Pitch	Soccer field
Rubbish	Garbage
Telly	Television

When David was ten, he went away to his first sleepaway soccer camp, called the Bobby Charlton Soccer and Sports Academy. The camp was in Manchester—about four hours from David's hometown. Bobby Charlton was one of the best soccer players of all time and had played for Manchester United.

Bobby Charlton

At first, David was homesick. He called home and pretended he had a toothache. He asked his parents to come get him. Instead, his mom and dad encouraged their son to stay. David ended up loving his time at camp enough to go back the following year.

"David's love of football was more important than any worries about missing mum or dad," his father explained.

The second summer at the camp, David, now eleven, became "winner of the week." This meant that he was named the best player in the entire camp. It also meant he would compete in a skills competition against the overall winners from the other weeks of camp. David was amazing on the day of the competition. He was an artist with the ball, making it do whatever he wanted. He was more skilled than any other boy there. Other parents watching that day kept coming up to David's mom and dad. "Is that your lad?" they would ask. "The little blond kid? He's fantastic! Absolutely brilliant!"

David was the overall winner! The prize was a two-week trip to Barcelona, Spain, to watch Fútbol Club Barcelona's training sessions, and to play with the club. FC Barcelona is a professional Spanish soccer team. Despite David being so young, his skills made an impression on the Barcelona coach right away.

"I knew from the first time I saw him that David Beckham would be something special," the coach said. "I must have watched thousands of kids in my time, but as we said goodbye I made sure I would not forget his name."

CHAPTER 3
Leaving Home

David's thirteenth birthday was on May 2, 1988. On that day, David and his mom and dad had lunch with Alex Ferguson, the manager of Manchester United. Scouts from the team had been watching David play over the last couple years.

They had also seen him win best overall player at summer camp. (A scout is a person who travels all over to watch young athletes play. They evaluate them to see if any of the players are good enough and the right fit for their team.)

"David was totally different," one scout said. "We all thought he was a brilliant person and polite and thoughtful as well as highly professional." Many scouts knew how special David was, and they wanted to make him part of their program.

Manchester United offered David a contract to play for them for the next six years. The first two years of the contract he would play for United and stay in school. This meant he would still live at home and play for his other teams. But he would train with Manchester's youth teams over the summer months. After two years, he would move to Manchester full-time and play as a trainee. Then, after that, David would hopefully be good enough to play on their elite team.

David was thrilled about the signing. He had only just turned thirteen, but this was the moment he had been waiting for his whole life.

"I want to sign," he said within minutes after the meeting began.

After the signing was over, David and his mom and dad had a three-hour car ride back home. David's head was in the clouds the whole way.

Manchester United and the Premier League

Manchester United is one of the wealthiest and most famous sports teams in the entire world. It is also the most popular. It has an estimated 50 million fans and more than two hundred official fan clubs. The team is estimated to be worth close to $4 billion. It has won the English top division championship twenty times as of 2018.

Manchester United is one of twenty teams that play in the Premier League, which is the top level of soccer in England. It is the most watched league of any sport. Premier League games are broadcast to more than a billion homes in 188 countries around the world.

"I don't remember us driving back to London at all," David later admitted. "I'd just lived through the happiest day of my life."

The next two years seemed almost magical to David. He continued to play on his local teams and then played for United during the summer months. He stayed in a giant dorm room with other young exceptional players. He loved every minute of it. When David was about fifteen and a half, he moved to Manchester full-time to begin his days as a trainee. After signing with United, it was clear that soccer was his future. In Manchester, he stayed with a couple who hosted young soccer players. David's new home was so close to the United training ground, he could see the soccer fields from his bedroom window. The couple's own son was grown, so they had spare bedrooms. They treated David as if he was their own.

"They were like a second mum and dad," David said about his hosts, "so loving and caring."

David's own mom and dad came to Manchester every weekend to visit and see their son play.

CHAPTER 4
A Pro at Last

Practicing with professionals, David became a better and better player. He was surrounded by other players who wanted to be a star as much as he did. Brothers Philip and Gary Neville had also signed with United around the same time David did. They all became close friends.

"Apart from loving soccer and wanting to play for United, there were things in our backgrounds that brought us together as well," David said. "Gary and Phil's mum and dad, for example, were so much like my parents."

David was now six feet tall and weighed 165 pounds. He was still thin. David made up for his slight build by practicing harder than his teammates. If there was an extra training session, David never missed it. He lived on the soccer field. David's position was midfield. This means he was expected to contribute on both offense and defense, running up to nine miles around the field during every ninety-minute game.

Manchester United Class of 1992

The midfield position was perfect for David because he was so good on offense and on defense. He could kick the ball long distances or curve it exactly where he wanted it to go. He could make perfect passes that slipped right in between defenders and landed directly at a teammate's feet.

On September 23, 1992, David made his first
professional appearance with Manchester United.
He was seventeen years old. When he was called
into the game, he was so excited that he hit his
head on the dugout roof when he jumped off the
bench. It was a night game and David played for

just seventeen minutes. After the game, some of the United coaches thought David still needed time to become even better. It would take another couple years until he made the first team for good.

Manchester United has other teams besides their main one. They have an under-eighteen team and an under-twenty-three team. These teams aren't nearly as good as the first team. David played on these teams for the next couple years. During the 1994–95 season, he was pulled into some first-team United games, but only when the regular starters needed rest. He scored his first goal for United on December 7, 1994, in a game against Galatasaray, a team from Turkey. United won easily, 4–0, but David's goal was one of the highlights. The announcer called him "that youngster Beckham." Nobody knew quite yet, but that youngster would soon be a world-famous soccer star.

Soccer Positions

A professional soccer game is played with eleven players on each of two teams: ten field players and one goalie. A goalkeeper is the only player on the field who is allowed to use their hands—but only when inside their team's penalty area. The goalkeeper tries to keep the ball out of the goal, and is also in charge of directing their team's defenders.

Within the ten field players, there are usually four defenders, who try to stop the other team from scoring. There are three midfielders, who defend their goal and try to score on their opponent's goal, too. Midfielders have to be in top shape because they do a lot of running.

Finally, there are three forwards, who try to score on their opponent's goal. Sometimes teams change how many players are on offense or defense. It depends where a team's strengths and weaknesses are, as well as the formation of the other team.

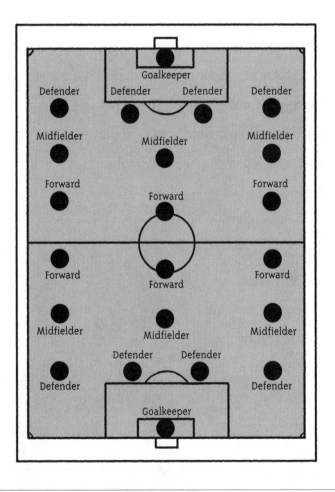

CHAPTER 5
The Making of a Star

During the 1995–96 season, David, now twenty, began starting for Manchester United regularly. David wasn't only growing up on the field, but off the field, too. He bought his own home, and it was a ten-minute drive from the stadium!

During David's first season as a full-time starter, United won the Premier League championship. He scored eight goals over the entire season and was becoming pretty well known in England. When people saw him on the street, they'd say to him, "Well done, Becks," or "Great goal, David."

1995/1996 Premier League champions

It was the first game of the 1996–97 Premier League season that made David famous around the world. United was beating Wimbledon, 2–0,

with just minutes left on the clock. David was controlling the ball about sixty yards (more than half the field) away from his opponent's goal. He noticed that the goalkeeper had wandered way

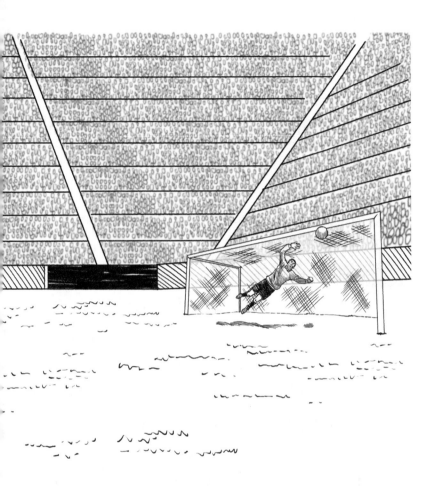

outside where he normally stands. David launched the ball with his right foot and it sailed through the air. The ball floated over the goalkeeper's head and right into the back of the net. *Gooooalllll!*

The crowd went crazy, and David's teammates jumped on him in glee. Soccer players didn't usually score a goal from that far out—even players as talented as David.

"It changed my life," David said later about the goal. "The ball seemed to be in the air for hours and all went quiet. Then the ball went in and the crowd just erupted. I was on cloud nine."

The fans at the game weren't the only ones who saw David's amazing goal. The head coach of England's national team noticed it, too. Less than a month after his astounding 1996 goal, David was asked to play for the national team. This was an even bigger deal than playing for United. England had twenty top professional teams, but only one national team. "It was an amazing feeling at twenty-one," David said about being picked. "I would be lying if I said I hadn't thought about it, but you don't dare to get your hopes up too much."

CHAPTER 6
The Spice of His Life

David now played for Manchester United *and* for England's national team. Everything in David's life revolved around soccer. He played all day long and dreamed about it at night. But that was about to change when he met Victoria Adams. Victoria's

Victoria Adams

professional name was Posh Spice, and she was a member of the music group the Spice Girls.

David met Victoria when she came to watch a United game during the 1996–97 season. Although David and

Victoria only spoke briefly, they liked each other instantly. A few weeks later, they went on their first date. Because Victoria was so famous, they couldn't just go out to any restaurant for dinner. Instead, they simply drove around and talked. Victoria was leaving for the United States the next day to go on tour with the Spice Girls. She promised she would call David once she reached New York.

The Spice Girls

The Spice Girls are one of the most famous female singing groups of all time. Five supercool British women formed the group in 1994. In 1996 they released their first single, "Wannabe." The song hit number one on the pop charts in thirty-seven countries. Their first album, *Spice*, sold more than 31 million copies around the world—the most albums sold by any female pop group ever.

The women in the group had fun nicknames— Posh Spice (Victoria Adams, now Beckham), Scary

 Spice (Melanie Brown), Baby Spice (Emma Bunton), Sporty Spice (Melanie Chisholm), and Ginger Spice (Geri Halliwell). They were

an extremely popular group, and the women were constantly mobbed by their fans. The band broke up in 2000, but has reunited since then for special concerts and events.

Victoria and David soon began spending hours talking on the phone while she was traveling from city to city. David's cell phone bill was as high as $2,000 a month! He sent flowers to every hotel Victoria stayed in while on tour.

When the Spice Girls' tour was over and David and Victoria could finally go out together,

fans and photographers followed them everywhere. She was a beautiful pop star. He was a handsome and stylish athlete. People wanted to know all about them. Victoria was used to this type of attention, but it was more than David had encountered when he was on his own.

"I couldn't believe the fuss," David admitted.

"Flashbulbs [from cameras] popping everywhere we went, stories all over the papers almost every day, and everyone having an opinion on us and our lives."

David proposed to Victoria on January 24, 1998. She said yes right away. The engaged couple even had their own nickname: Posh & Becks.

David was now as famous for being Posh Spice's fiancé as he was for being an awesome soccer player. They were officially one of the world's favorite couples.

CHAPTER 7
The Villain

During the summer of 1998, David and England's national team were getting ready to play in the World Cup in France. Thirty-two national teams would play in the world final. England had not qualified for the last World Cup tournament, in 1994. This time around, English fans were desperate for their team to do well.

England was set to play Argentina on June 30. Only the winner would move on.

About 30,600 fans watched the game in the stadium, and back in England, 23 million— almost half the country—watched the game on television. The score was tied at the beginning of the second half, when a player from Argentina, Diego Simeone, ran up and knocked David down from behind. David was frustrated and mad about being hit. As Diego walked by him, when he was still on the ground, David lost his temper. He kicked Diego. Diego fell to the ground.

The World Cup

The World Cup is a soccer tournament held every four years between thirty-two national teams from countries around the world. Games are played before it begins to decide which teams get to participate. The World Cup lasts several weeks.

It is the most watched sporting event in the world!

A different country hosts each time. Since the first World Cup in 1930, England has won once, in 1966. Brazil has won the most titles, with five.

The Women's World Cup was first held in 1991. Since then, the United States has won the most women's titles (four), including their win in 2019.

The kick didn't hurt Diego, but it was still the wrong thing for David to do. The referee gave David a red card. When an official gives a player a red card, this means the player must leave the game, and their team is not allowed to replace them with a substitute. England's team was forced to play the rest of the game with only ten players. The second half ended in a 2–2 tie. This meant that the game would be decided by penalty kicks. England lost, 4–3. They had been knocked out of the World Cup.

English fans blamed David for the loss. They thought if he had not gotten a red card, England would have won the game. The headline of one newspaper the next day read WHAT AN IDIOT! Another paper called David a spoiled brat.

Billboards with David's picture on them were torn down across the country. David was extremely upset by how mad everybody was. He knew his country loved soccer and wanted to win, but he didn't realize *how badly* they wanted to win.

"This is without a doubt the worst moment of my career. I will always regret my actions," David said. "I want every English supporter to know how sorry I am."

His apology didn't seem to matter. The whole country had gone from loving David Beckham to hating David Beckham. David left for the United States, where Victoria was on tour with the Spice Girls. When Victoria saw David, she gave him the biggest hug in the world. She spoke out in his defense. "He more than anyone wanted England to go all the way," said Victoria.

CHAPTER 8
United Behind David

David returned from America to England in mid-July 1998 to start training with Manchester United for the upcoming season. David did nothing else besides play soccer. When he went out, he dressed in black and kept a hoodie up over his head. He didn't want anybody to recognize him. It didn't work. He still had to have police officers escort him places to protect him from angry fans. "I think it might be hard for people to understand what it was like living my life in those first months after the World Cup," David said.

David's United teammates, including Phil and Gary Neville, and his coaches stuck by him and told him to hold his head high. The United coach signed David to a new five-year, $6 million contract to show how committed they were to their star. "Don't worry about what anyone says," David's coach said. "You can have your say back to the rest of them after the season begins."

David did just that: In United's first game of the 1998–99 season, they were down 2–1. David was granted a free kick, which is one of the things he does best. He can make the ball move any way he likes. The 60,000 fans in the stadium stood up to cheer. On this shot, David bent the ball around a wall of defenders and landed it into a corner of the goal. The crowd erupted in cheers.

"I knew exactly what I wanted to say to the United supporters above the roar," David said later. "Thank you for standing by me. That goal is for you."

David still had to face angry fans when his team traveled to other stadiums. Fans of the other team jeered every time he touched the ball. Sometimes fans would throw things like trash or

bottles at him. David just did what he did best—
he played soccer.

During the 1998–99 season, Manchester
United won three different championships.
In addition to winning the Premier League
Championship, United won the FA Cup and the
UEFA Champions League. Winning all three in
a single season is called winning the "treble of
trophies."

The Treble of Trophies

The three important championships that make up the treble of trophies are the Premier League Championship, the Football Association (FA) Challenge Cup, and the Union of European Football Associations (UEFA) European Cup. The FA Cup is a knockout tournament, which almost any club in England can enter. The UEFA Champions League is a competition among the best professional soccer teams in all of Europe.

The Champions League final is the most watched sporting event in the world every year when the World Cup isn't being played.

The 1998-99 season was the first time Manchester United were the champions of Europe since 1968. When the Manchester United team arrived home to their city, more than half a million people lined the streets to congratulate them. The season, David later said,

"started with me not sure about whether I'd make it through to the following May in one piece. It ended up being the most incredible season any of us—maybe any soccer player in this country—will ever experience."

In March of that season, David and Victoria's first child was born. They named him Brooklyn

Joseph. In his son's honor, David got a tattoo of Brooklyn's name on his lower back. Soon afterward, he also got a guardian angel tattoo above the name. He wanted his son to feel protected.

In July 1999, Victoria and David were married in a castle in Ireland. The couple sat on gold thrones as they took their vows. Gary Neville was his best man. Their wedding cake was so tall, it had to be cut with a sword! David wore a white suit during the ceremony, and Victoria wore a beautiful white wedding dress. Afterward, the couple changed into matching purple outfits.

The next day, David and Victoria traveled to the South of France for their honeymoon. They stayed for just one week, though. After all, another soccer season was about to start.

CHAPTER 9
Forgiven

After David and Victoria got married, they continued to get a lot of attention. Some soccer fans were still mad at David for his World Cup mistake, but it seemed like everybody wanted to know *everything* about "Posh & Becks" and their baby, Brooklyn.

Beckingham Palace

The couple bought a seven-bedroom mansion in England with an indoor pool. Because the queen of England lives in Buckingham Palace, newspapers called their new home "*Beck*ingham Palace." It certainly looked as though David and Victoria lived like royalty, too.

When David wasn't wearing a soccer uniform, he always dressed well. He liked to wear suits and leather jackets with designer labels like Gucci. He also liked to wear casual clothes from brands like Adidas. Young men started to dress like David. They wore their hair like David. If he shaved his head, teenagers around the world shaved their heads. If he wore a knit cap, soon his many fans were wearing knit caps, too. David made it cool for boys to dress stylishly and to care about what they looked like. "Maybe I've affected people's style, or their having certain haircuts," David said. "I didn't do it for attention. I did it because that was just me."

David and Victoria began going to fashion shows and celebrity parties. They appeared in ads for clothes, cologne, and perfume. They became good friends with other celebrities, including Elton John, one of the most famous performers in the world.

On the soccer field, David and Manchester United continued to win. They won the Premier League Championship title three years in a row: 1999, 2000, and 2001.

David was also named captain of England's national team—one of the country's highest honors. "I was frozen to my spot when I heard," David said later. "I was so excited, so proud, humbled by just the thought of it."

The English team was getting ready to play in the 2002 World Cup, held in South Korea and Japan. After what happened in the 1998 World Cup, David couldn't wait to prove himself this time around. And now he could do it as the team leader.

2002 World Cup logo

Team Captain

The captain of a national soccer team is a leader both on and off the field. Sometimes called skipper, the captain wears an armband during games so officials can identify them.

The captain's only "official" job is to call the coin toss prior to the start of the game. Unofficially, though, the skipper sets an example of how to play the game and how to behave when not playing. David was a captain for England for 115 games.

England faced Argentina again in the opening round of the World Cup tournament. Newspapers called the match a "revenge game" for David. The game was tied 0–0 in the first half, when a foul occurred. David got to take a penalty kick.

"I've never felt such pressure before," said David later about this kick. "Everything was swirling around me, every nerve standing on edge."

David ran forward and kicked the ball as hard as he could. *Gooooooalllll!!!*

There were no more goals after that. The game ended 1–0.

"What had happened in 1998 had done a lot to make me the person I'd become," David said. "But with one kick, it was all off my shoulders for good."

England loses to Brazil in World Cup quarterfinals, 2002

England made it all the way to the quarterfinals, where they lost to the eventual champions, Brazil. David and all of England had hoped to win the title, but it didn't happen. David, though, remained team captain for four more years. And best of all, he felt like he had made things right. His time as his country's most hated player was officially over for good.

CHAPTER 10
United No More

After the World Cup, David went back to training with United. He also became a dad once again. He and Victoria had their second son, Romeo James, on September 1, 2002. David got another tattoo on his back of his new son's name. Because David was a worldwide celebrity, even something as small as a new tattoo was big news around the world. David had business deals to represent Armani clothing, Ray-Ban sunglasses, and even Pepsi. He was paid a lot of money to appear in advertisements for these companies. He always seemed to be on the covers of many different magazines. "He represents something for every woman," said the editor of *Marie Claire*, a women's magazine.

"Father, husband, footballer, icon. In a word, he's the ultimate hero."

In 2002, a movie premiered that showed how very popular David was all over the world. His name was right there in the title: *Bend It Like Beckham*!

Alex Ferguson

There was one person who wasn't a fan of all the attention on David: his Manchester United coach, Alex Ferguson. Alex had managed the team since 1986, and he was beginning to think David was spending too much time on endorsing products and going to celebrity parties and not enough time on soccer. David thought he could do both. They disagreed on this point.

At the end of the season, United won the Premier League Championship again, the sixth of David's career. David, twenty-eight, was still one of the best players in the world, but he wouldn't be on United much longer. Although Alex thought David was a wonderful player, he wasn't comfortable coaching someone as famous as David.

"I felt uncomfortable with the celebrity aspect of his life," Alex said.

Bend It Like Beckham

Bend It Like Beckham is a 2002 movie about an eighteen-year-old girl named Jesminder, played by Parminder Kaur Nagra, who loves soccer. She is a David Beckham superfan. Her parents don't approve of her playing soccer, so she plays in secret.

The title of the movie comes from the way  David Beckham can make the ball curve when he kicks it. He can make the ball travel (it appears to bend) around defenders. Jess wishes she could do that, too.

This comedy about women's soccer was a big hit.

In the summer of 2003, Manchester United released David's contract. This meant he was no longer on the team. David was free to sign with another squad. This was a big deal. David had been a part of United since he was thirteen years old. He thought he would play for them his entire career.

"I was United, born and bred," he said.

But not anymore. David soon found his new team. He became only the third British player to join Real (say: REE-al) Madrid, one of the best teams in Spain and even throughout Europe. He signed for over $30 million.

A big chapter in David's life had ended, but an exciting new one was about to begin.

"I will always hold precious memories of my time at Manchester United as well as of the players," David reflected. "But I know I have been given a great opportunity. Real is a remarkable club, after all."

Real Madrid CF

Founded in 1902, Real Madrid Club de Fútbol plays in Spain's top league, called La Liga. Real has won more La Liga championships—thirty-three—than any other team. *Real* means "royal" in Spanish.

They were the best European team of the twentieth century. They have had many famous players compete for them, including Ronaldo, from Brazil (2002–2007), Cristiano Ronaldo, from Portugal (2009–2018), and Zinedine Zidane, of France (2001–2006). Zinedine has been a coach with Real Madrid since 2014.

CHAPTER 11
Hola! (Hello!) and Adios! (Goodbye!)

On August 30, 2003, David made his debut with Real Madrid. Fans wanted to see whether he was worth all the money and hype that came with having such a big celebrity on their team.

There was a lot of pressure on him. But, as British fans might say, David was brilliant! He scored a goal in his first game, and Madrid won, 2–1. David's career in Spain was off to a blazing start.

Spanish fans loved having David on the Real Madrid team and his family in Spain. But did they love them *too* much? David and Victoria hired bodyguards to protect themselves and their children from all the photographers who followed them and surrounded them, hoping to sell the photographs to magazines, newspapers, and websites for money. And now

David and Victoria had an even larger family to protect. In February 2005, the Beckhams' third son, Cruz David, was born. Of course, David had his new son's name tattooed on his back along with his two other children's names.

Even though David was playing for a professional team in Spain now, he was still captain of England's national team.

England was one of the thirty-two teams who made it to the 2006 World Cup in Germany. But they lost to Portugal in the quarterfinals.

David, at age thirty-one, decided it was time to step down as England's captain.

"It has been an honor and a privilege to have captained our country," David said. "I have lived the dream. I am extremely proud to have worn the armband and been captain of England, and for that I will always be grateful."

During David's fourth season with Madrid, he helped the team win a league championship. But just as his time as captain of England's national team came to an end, he felt ready to leave Spain, too. David, now thirty-two, left Madrid after four years and signed with the Los Angeles Galaxy, a Major League Soccer team in the United States.

91

Pro Soccer in North America

The top men's professional soccer league in the United States and Canada is Major League Soccer (MLS). Its first season was in 1996 and had ten teams competing. Today it has twenty-one teams in the United States and three in Canada. The champion of the league every year wins the MLS Cup.

The women's professional soccer league in the United States is the National Women's Soccer League. It began play in 2013 and has nine teams across the country.

CHAPTER 12
Welcome to the United States

Soccer is the most popular sport around the world, but most Americans like football, basketball, and baseball much better. David wanted to change this. "I am attempting to take the sport into the mainstream," David said about his move to America. "I am a player, but also an ambassador." As ambassador, David wanted to "sell" soccer. He wanted Americans to play it,

watch it, and care about it as much as the rest of the world does.

Even if people in the United States didn't seem to be huge soccer fans yet, they definitely knew who David was. He and Victoria planned to spend a lot of their time modeling and continuing to develop their advertising and endorsement deals. They knew Los Angeles, where so many other celebrities lived, would be a great place to do it. "I knew the lifestyle was going to fit me and Victoria and the kids," David said. "It is a chance to make my mark not just on a new club, but a new country."

When David and his family arrived in Los Angeles in July 2007, the airport was packed with fans, reporters, and photographers waiting to get a glimpse of the Beckham family. The city hosted a private party welcoming them to Los Angeles. Many famous celebrities attended, including actors Tom Cruise and Will Smith. More than seven hundred reporters and five thousand fans showed up at the ceremony presenting David as a player for the Galaxy for the first time.

David earned a lot of money to play for the Galaxy, and if he helped the team win championships, he would make even more.

Once in the States, in addition to posing for other people's ads, David began his own companies. He had his own brand of cologne and even underwear. He was paid to promote the Walt Disney theme parks. He and Victoria appeared on the covers of dozens of  American magazines. The Beckham brand was making a major mark on the United States.

More than 300,000 of David's Galaxy jersey sold in his first season. It was the most popular athletic jersey in the world that year.

But David's first and second seasons on the soccer field were a disappointment. David was often injured and the Galaxy struggled. In his last two seasons, David led the Galaxy to back-to-back MLS titles in 2011 and 2012.

David and Victoria also had their fourth child and first daughter while they were living in California. Harper Seven Beckham was born on July 10, 2011. Seven was the number David

wore for Manchester United as well as for the English national team. Just as David had done for his three boys, he got a tattoo of his daughter's name, this time on his neck. David played his final match with the Galaxy on December 1, 2012. The team beat the Houston Dynamo to win the championship, 3–1. The sold-out crowd of 30,510 in Los Angeles gave David a standing ovation.

CHAPTER 13
Mission Accomplished?

David's time playing in the United States did make him more famous, but it didn't boost MLS's popularity enough to compete for American fans with professional football, basketball, or baseball. Whenever David played, whether home or away, the stadium was filled. But Americans still didn't watch MLS games on television. David saw that Americans weren't embracing soccer yet, but he wasn't ready to give up. "I may not play here anymore," David said after his last game. "But I remain just as committed to growing this club, this league, and this sport."

David, now thirty-seven, still had one soccer season to play, though. He signed with Paris Saint-Germain, a professional team in France.

Between his salary, his own brands, and his other business endorsements, David was one of the world's highest-paid athletes, earning more than $46 million. So instead of keeping his new team salary, he donated the $3 million to a local children's charity.

David joined Paris Saint-Germain after their season had already started. He played five months with them until the season ended. He then retired from the game for good. His last game was on May 18, 2013, where he had one assist, off a corner kick. Paris Saint-Germain won the French league title. Every professional team David had ever played on had won a championship in his final season with them. "I had always wanted to go out on top, and by winning the French League, I had achieved just that," he said. "It feels right to be retiring, but it also feels awful."

David played soccer his entire life, and at thirty-eight, his career was suddenly over. He was still one of the world's biggest celebrities and would continue to be so. But he wasn't a soccer player anymore; he was a *retired* soccer player.

David kept his promise about returning to America. In 2014, a year after his last game, David announced he would be one of the owners of a new MLS team, Inter Miami CF, in Miami, Florida. The team had their first matches in 2020.

David and Victoria are still celebrities in the United States and all over the world. Together they are worth more than a billion dollars! Victoria has her own clothing and makeup lines. David has his own brands of skin care products and fragrances. He also models clothing for many different companies. The Beckhams have established their own charity, which donates wheelchairs to kids in need. They also donate to other charities such as Help for Heroes, which assists wounded British veterans.

No matter how famous David becomes, he will always be passionate about soccer, or football, as he calls it. He has his jersey numbers, as well as the dates of other memorable years from his playing days, tattooed on his body. He says the sport will always be a part of him . . . and it will always be missed.

"There will be other challenges, other goals, other exciting things to look forward to," David says. "I have no doubt of that. I will always be centered by my family, who mean everything. But nothing will fully replace football. How could anything replace football?"

Timeline of David Beckham's Life

1975 — David Beckham is born in London, England, on May 2

1986 — Wins the overall skills competition at the Bobby Charlton Camp, and wins a two-week trip to Barcelona, Spain

1988 — Signs his first contract with Manchester United on May 2, his thirteenth birthday

1992 — Plays his first professional game with Manchester United on September 23

1996 — Wins his first Premier League Championship title in May; scores his famous sixty-yard goal the following August; makes his first national team appearance in September

1999 — David and Victoria (Posh Spice) Adams marry on July 4 at a castle in Ireland

2000 — David is appointed captain of England's national team

2003 — Leaves Manchester United and joins Real Madrid

2007 — Joins the Los Angeles Galaxy of Major League Soccer

2013 — Signs a five-month contract with Paris Saint-Germain in January; retires from soccer in May

2020 — David Beckham's team, Inter Miami CF, plays its first matches in Major League Soccer

Timeline of the World

1975 — Arthur Ashe becomes the first black man to win Wimbledon singles title

1979 — Margaret Thatcher becomes the first woman prime minister of Great Britain

1981 — Prince Charles marries Lady Diana Spencer on July 29

1983 — First commercial cell phone is sold on October 13

1989 — Disney—MGM Studios opens to the public at Walt Disney World

1990 — The Hubble Space Telescope is launched

1996 — The first Pokémon games are introduced on Nintendo Game Boy

2001 — The world's longest train (more than 4.5 miles) is set up to run in Western Australia

2005 — Pope John Paul II dies on April 2

2010 — A volcanic eruption in Iceland disrupts air travel throughout Northern and Western Europe

2016 — Great Britain votes to leave the European Union on June 20

2019 — The United States wins the Women's World Cup, held in France

Bibliography

*Books for young readers

Beckham, David. ***David Beckham.*** Headline Publishing Group:
London, 2013.

*Beckham, David. ***David Beckham's Soccer Skills.*** New York:
HarperCollins, 2006.

Beckham, David, with Dean Freeman (photographer). ***Beckham:
My World.*** Hodder and Stoughton: London, 2000.

Beckham, David, with Tom Watt. ***Beckham: Both Feet on the
Ground.*** HarperCollins: New York, 2003.

Beckham, David, with Tom Watt. ***David Beckham: My Side.***
CollinsWillow: London, 2003.

Beckham, Ted, with Tim Allan. ***David Beckham: My Son.***
Pan Books: London, 2005.

*Jökulsson, Illugi. ***Before They Were Stars: How Messi, Alex
Morgan, and Other Soccer Greats Rose to the Top.***
(World Soccer Legends). New York: Abbeville Kids, 2019.

Reavis, Tracey Savell. ***The Life and Career of David Beckham.***
Rowman & Littlefield: Plymouth, United Kingdom, 2014.

Russell, Gwen. ***Arise Sir David Beckham.*** John Blake Publishing:
London, 2007.

Wahl, Grant. ***The Beckham Experiment: How the World's Most
Famous Athlete Tried to Conquer America.*** Crown Publishers:
New York, 2009.